From Worries to Wisdom:

How to Unlock Your Potential to overcome Anxiety, Depression, Self-Sabotage & Overthinking

Published By:

AIC

Copyright © 2024. All rights reserved.

No part of this publication may be copied, reproduced in any format, by any means, electronic or otherwise, without prior consent from the copyright owner and publisher of this book.

From Worries to Wisdom

Contents

INTRODUCTION 4
CONCLUSION 23
ACKNOWLEDGEMENT 24

Introduction

In today's world, it's no secret that many of us are carrying heavy burdens struggling with work, family issues, and the overwhelming weight of mental health challenges like depression and anxiety. The COVID-19 pandemic has only made things tougher, with more people feeling hopeless and lost than ever before.

A Quranic surah holds the key to alleviating depression, overthinking, stress, and anxiety. The "Law of Attraction," offering simple methods to unlock the answers we seek. But what exactly is the law of attraction, and how does it relate to finding a solution for depression? But how can we comprehend its mechanisms?

To address these challenges, an 18th-century movement emerged with the aim of synthesizing global knowledge to find solutions to our problems.

Moreover, do the Quran and Hadith endorse this concept? And if so, what are the two simple methods that can effectively solve our problems? With curiosity and an open heart, we'll explore the hidden secret within a verse of Surah Najm and its connection to Law of Attraction.

In this book, join me on this journey of faith, discovery, and healing through a unique approach. Because within these pages lies the promise of brighter days ahead—a promise of hope and the strength to overcome any challenge that comes our way.

From Worries to Wisdom

I am certain that you are worried about something in your life. These are indeed tough times, especially after Covid-19, due to inflation. Everyone is troubled, but I know that your worries might extend beyond just inflation. You might be anxious about your future, financial difficulties, poverty, or maybe you or a family member is suffering from a chronic illness. It could even be that all these issues are present in your life simultaneously. With so many problems, it sometimes feels like we are battling a multi-headed monster. Sometimes, it seems as though we are on the verge of losing this fight, and the stress can lead us into depression. But the real question is, what is the solution to these problems?

In our subcontinent, particularly in Pakistani and Indian culture, a very famous method is often used to address worries. And surely, at some point in your life, you must have encountered this method. That method is reciting specific prayers or verses (Wazaif). Someone might have advised you at some point to recite a particular verse to solve your problems, get married, start a business, have children, etc. Whether these prayers work or not, I do not know, because I am neither a scholar nor a religious expert. Therefore, I am not going to tell you to recite a specific verse a certain number of times to solve your problem. Nor am I going to suggest any home remedies or meditation techniques, such as doing yoga or deep breathing exercises to reduce your stress. I am not an expert in those fields either.

However, there is one field where I have expertise. It is a field I have been studying for the past 11 years, although this study would have been of no use to me if God had not brought the answer to my question suddenly before me.

But before I present my research work to you, I would like to share some theories from other experts regarding solutions to problems, so you don't think I only consider my own views to be correct.

For example, let's talk about an illness that is currently growing faster than any other disease in the world: depression. One of the most dangerous diseases, because once a person is afflicted by it, he or she starts losing interest in everything else. He or she loses interest in their family, business, studies, and everything else. Data shows that the number of depression patients has more than doubled since Covid-19.

To understand the severity of depression, a test called BDI (Beck Depression Inventory) is conducted. This test consists of 21 questions and is currently the most widely used psychometric test. It indicates the severity of your anxiety or depression. However, the purpose of this book is not to discuss your problems but to provide you with your solutions.

If you ask a doctor for a solution to your anxiety or depression, they will give you mild sedatives, which are medications that numb your brain or certain parts of it, providing temporary relief.

If you ask a psychologist for a solution to your anxiety or depression, they will tell you to change your thinking, advising you not to focus too much on troubling thoughts and to try to stay happy.

There are several famous books on changing one's thinking, such as "The Power of Positive Thinking" by Norman Vincent Peale or the famous book by Napoleon Hill, "Think and Grow Rich," which is also quite well-known in its Urdu translation as "Sochain Aur Dolat Kamayen" ("Think and Earn Wealth"). However, I am not going to tell you to read any book.

There was a very special reason I mentioned this because I wanted to draw your attention to a specific word, and that word is "thinking." But what happens when you change your thinking? Does your problem disappear just because you stop thinking about it? No, nothing like that happens. Simply claiming that changing your thinking will make your problems disappear is not enough. Therefore, I did a little research on human thinking, and from the work done by Krista Taylor, I confirmed that there is indeed a connection between depression and our thinking patterns.

Let me tell you about an American watchmaker from the 18th century named Phineas Quimby, who was very famous for making watches. Phineas contracted an illness that we know today as TB (tuberculosis). You know that if TB is not treated, it can be fatal.

This was in the 18th century when there was no known cure for TB. So, Phineas started searching for ways to treat himself. He noticed that when he engaged in his favorite activity, which was horseback riding, he experienced great excitement and happiness. During these moments of great joy, he temporarily found relief from his illness. Consequently, he concluded that the real essence is the heart and mind; the body is merely a dwelling place for them. If the heart and mind are healthy, the body will function properly on its own.

Phineas became so convinced of this idea that he began spreading his ideas to others. This marked the beginning of a new philosophy, which you and I know today as the Law of Attraction.

These days, this word is very popular among the educated class. The basic meaning of the Law of Attraction is that the kind of thoughts you think will manifest in your life. Human thoughts are like energy, and just as one form of energy attracts another similar form, positive thoughts will attract positive events and experiences around you.

The concept of the Law of Attraction was very intriguing to the world, leading many people to start investigating whether it truly exists. Can positive thinking or hopeful expectations really alleviate our worries?

To find the answer to this question, believers in the Law of Attraction did something remarkable: they decided to compile all the knowledge from human history in one place and see what great wisdom would emerge, and what it could teach us about overcoming life's challenges.

So, they gathered all ancient philosophies, such as those of the ancient Greeks, ancient Egyptians, Roman Empire knowledge and skills, Chinese texts, Vedic literature, and teachings of ancient religions. From these, they extracted the most fundamental and common elements. And now, I am going to present that essence to you. Every word I am about to write is very measured, and you need to read carefully because this is a turning point in my research. They concluded that:

There is an infinite power, an infinite energy. It is the greatest, more powerful than anything else, omnipresent, and eternal. Some people call it God, but we cannot fully comprehend it as it is beyond human understanding. However, if we somehow align ourselves with this power, or tune in to it, and believe in it, it will free us from all our difficulties.

This concept was very interesting to me because if the essence of all the world's knowledge includes the word "God," then it is very likely that the solution to all problems might be found in religion. The statement I just shared with you, if you think about it, contains some words that exactly resemble God or God's attributes, such as an infinite power, an omnipresent and eternal force.

However, there is one question that this statement does not answer: how can we tune ourselves to this force or God? How can we align ourselves with it so that it resolves all our problems?

For this, we need to look at the source given to us by God, which is the holy scriptures. But holy scriptures often seem to contain mostly commandments, such as do this and don't do that. My goal is to find a solution to the problem. How can we find answers to our questions from a book of commandments? There is a way, and to explain it, I want to take you to 15th century Jerusalem for a moment.

In the Ottoman Empire's Palestine, there was a Jewish scholar named Isaac Luria. He started a new interpretation of the Torah based on its four layers.

The first layer, Peshat, refers to the simple or literal meaning of the text.

The second layer, Remez, points to the hints or implied messages within the verse.

The third layer, Derash, is about the lessons or moral teachings we can derive from the verse.

The fourth layer, Sort, deals with the hidden or secret meanings embedded within the verse.

There is no doubt that Isaac Luria made significant contributions to the interpretation of the Torah. But the question arises: can this method be applied to other holy scriptures, such as the Quran?

From Worries to Wisdom

To explore this, I would like to present to you verses 124 and 125 of Surah Al-Tawbah:

"When a Surah is revealed, the hypocrites ask, 'Which of you has this increased in faith?' As for those who believe, it has increased them in faith, and they rejoice. But as for those whose hearts have disease, it has only increased them in wickedness upon their wickedness, and they die as disbelievers."

Did you notice something? There are multiple layers of understanding. From the same Surah, some people gain faith while others derive disbelief. Different people interpret the same verse at different levels and in different ways. This implies that the verses of the Quran can also be interpreted in layers, revealing various hidden meanings. This is a crucial point because it is from here that I will provide you with a solution to your problems.

Take, for example, verse 39 of Surah Al-Najm:

"And that there is not for man except that [good] for which he strives."

How do you interpret this verse? A common person might understand it at the most basic layer, interpreting it to mean that if you strive for good deeds, you will be rewarded, and if you strive for bad deeds, you will be punished. This is how any ordinary person might interpret this verse.

However, Imam Shafi'i and his followers interpreted this verse at the second and third layers. They considered what the verse hints at and the lesson it teaches. From this interpretation, Imam Shafi'i derived a jurisprudential issue, explaining that the verse tells us that the rewards of Quran recitation do not reach the deceased because they did not strive for it, while the rewards of their offspring's prayers do reach them.

This is mentioned in a hadith from Jami` Al-Tirmidhi (1376),

"For indeed, the child is the result of one's own efforts."

You can see how multiple layers of interpretation can be applied to a single verse. If you allow me, I would like to present a fourth interpretation of this verse that is hidden, concealed: that for each person is what they strive for. You will get what you strive for. If you strive to improve your thinking, you will receive better outcomes.

This means that the Quran confirms the law of attraction. If you do not believe me, read the next verse (An-Najm 40-41):

"That his effort is going to be seen. Then he will be recompensed for it with the fullest recompense."

From Worries to Wisdom

Doesn't it seem like we are being told here that whatever effort you put in, you will receive the same in return? Those who strive for positive thoughts will receive the best outcomes in return. That is the law of attraction.

But where is the answer to our worries hidden in this? The answer to our worries is hidden in the next verses.

If you are worried about something, look at the next verse (An-Najm 43-53):

"And that He is the One who makes one laugh and weep."

If your worry is the loss of a loved one, see the next verse (An-Najm 44-53):

"And He is the One who causes death and gives life."

If your worry is about not having children, see the next verse (An-Najm 45-46):

"And that He created the pairs, male and female, from a sperm-drop when it is emitted."

If your worry is poverty and lack of wealth, see the next verse (An-Najm 48):

"And that it is He who enriches and suffices."

Do you see how our thinking is being tuned? It tells us that whatever effort you put in; you will receive the same in return. In times of grief, have faith in your Lord, for He is the one who will give you joy. Strive to be patient when separated from loved ones, because He is the one who gives life and death. Do not grieve over not having children, strive for belief because He is the one who grants children. Do not worry about wealth and poverty. Instead, have faith in Him because He is the one who enriches and suffices. You need to keep your faith in Allah and align your thinking in such a way that He will solve our problems and relieve us from our worries.

And regarding this certainty, the Prophet Muhammad (peace be upon him) also conveyed the same message.

(Musnad Ahmad #5605, Silsilah as-Saheehah #2738): "When you ask Allah, ask with the certainty that your request will be accepted. Allah does not accept the prayer of a servant who prays with a careless and heedless heart."

Maintain a mindset of certainty, believing that the One you are asking from will surely grant it to you and solve your problems. You may recall that I mentioned that this teaching of certainty has been imparted in all the philosophies throughout human history. I want to give you another piece of evidence that I found in the Bible.

(Book of Mark 11:24) When Jesus (peace be upon him) entered Jerusalem, he saw some people buying and selling in the Temple. Jesus (peace be upon him) became angry and said, "Have you turned the house of God into a den of thieves?" Then he drove the traders out of the Temple. After this, Jesus (peace be upon him) was preaching to his disciples and told them something very special: "When you pray, believe that you will receive it, and it will be yours." Ask for the solution to your problems with certainty.

Now, I want to tell you something very special. The law of attraction states that there is a powerful force, whose power has no limits, that is infinite. And if we tune ourselves to this force, it will solve all our problems. But the law of attraction does not tell us what this force is. This question remains a mystery for the law of attraction. However, in these verses from Surah Al-Najm, there are far more secrets revealed than in the law of attraction. And among these secrets is the identification of this force.

In the verses that immediately follow (Al-Najm 49),

"And that He is the Lord of Sirius."

If you read these verses together, you will notice something strange. Generally, these verses tell us that He makes one laugh and cry. He gives life and death. He grants children and wealth. Believe in this, and it will be granted to you. But then suddenly, a verse appears saying, "And that He is the Lord of Sirius." Isn't it a bit strange to suddenly mention a star? Initially, it talks about similar things: life, death, children, sustenance, wealth, blessings, but then it abruptly states that He is the Lord of Sirius. What do you know about Sirius?

AIC

Sirius is the name of a star, and it is not just any star but the brightest star in the night sky.

Remember, I told you about the multiple layers of interpretation of the verses. In the first layer, the literal meaning, this verse simply means that all the great stars in the sky were created by Him. This is the common understanding for the average person. But I do not just want to convey the literal meaning to you. I want to take you deeper and tell you about the fourth layer of this verse, which is called a secret: the hidden secret in this verse.

What is so special about the star Sirius that it suddenly appears in these verses? To understand the hidden secret behind the mention of the star Sirius, I studied information about it spanning the last four thousand years. I found that throughout history, the star Sirius has been given over 50 different names. For example,

The ancient Egyptians named it "Al-Habor," meaning the Dog's Head, which might seem like a meaningless name to you. But if you have studied Egyptian mythology, you would know that "Anubis," who had the head of a dog, was a deity for the ancient Egyptians. Thus, the star Sirius was a representation of their deity.

In India, the Sanskrit name for Sirius is "Mrigav yadha," meaning the Hunter of the Deer, which is another name for the Hindu god "Rudra" or "Shiva." Thus, Sirius was a representation of their deity.

From Worries to Wisdom

In the Malayalam language of South India, Sirius is called "Makar Jyoti," which is worshiped in the Sabarimala temple and represents a deity.

In Scandinavian countries, including Norway, Sweden, and Denmark, Sirius is called "Lokabrenna," meaning like Loki, who was a deity in Norse mythology.

In medieval Europe and the Arab world, Sirius was one of the 15 stars used for magic.

In "Zoroastrianism," one of the oldest religions, the sacred text "Avesta" refers to Sirius as a divine arrow, symbolizing a deity.

In the cultures of Senegal and Mauritania, Sirius is called "Yoonir," representing the entire universe.

After reading all this information, do you notice a pattern? "He is the Lord of Sirius,"—what secret is hidden in this? It means to believe in Him because.

"He is the Lord of your deities as well."

He has always been there. He solved the problems of those before you, and He will solve yours as well. But who is He? What is this force that we must believe in to end our worries? You will find the answer at the beginning of these verses (An-Najm 36-37):

" Or has he not been informed of what is in the Scripture of Moses, and ⌐that of⌐ Abraham, who ⌐perfectly⌐ fulfilled ⌐his covenant⌐?

At this point, I want to read to you a message given four thousand years ago, which was first sent to Abraham (peace be upon him), then to Moses (peace be upon him), and the same message was recited by David (peace be upon him) in the mountains, with the mountains echoing in praise. This message is written in the Torah, and I want you to read it as well. (Torah - Deuteronomy 6:4-9):

"Hear, O Israel: The Lord our God, the Lord is one. Love the Lord your God with all your heart and with all your soul and with all your strength."

You will find this same message in Islam as well, five times a day:

"I bear witness that there is no deity except Allah. I bear witness that there is no deity except Allah."

This is the deity in whom we must place our hopeful trust, believing that He will solve our problems. And how do we express this belief? We need to make a small acknowledgment before Him, and the Prophet Muhammad (peace be upon him) himself taught us this acknowledgment. Let me read it to you word for word:

From Worries to Wisdom

"O Allah, You are my Lord. There is no deity except You. You created me, and I am Your servant. I am trying my best to fulfill my covenant and promise to You. I acknowledge my sins. I acknowledge Your blessings upon me. So forgive me, for none but You can forgive sins."

You know that the Prophet Muhammad (peace be upon him) said,

"Whoever recites these words of supplication with a heart full of certainty and then dies during the day, will be among the people of Paradise before the evening. And if he dies during the night, he will be among the people of Paradise before the morning."

This is the original law of attraction: believe that He can alleviate our troubles, and only He can.

In Musnad Ahmad (13168), Safwan narrates that he was with Abdullah ibn Umar (may Allah be pleased with him). A man came and asked, "On the Day of Judgment, will Allah speak to His servant privately? Have you ever heard anything about this from the Prophet?" Abdullah replied, "Yes, Allah will bring His servant close to Him, place His hand over him, and conceal him from the people. Then He will ask, 'Do you remember such and such sin? Do you remember such and such sin?' The servant will acknowledge all his sins and think that he is doomed. But then Allah will say, 'I concealed these sins for you in the world, and today I forgive them all for you.'"

This is a Lord who is alone, who is the deity of all, who is unique, and who conceals my sins. Why wouldn't I believe in Him and pray to Him, knowing that He can alleviate all my troubles?

Conclusion

The journey we have taken through the pages of this book has revealed the profound connection between our thoughts, our faith, and our ability to overcome life's challenges. By understanding the power of our minds and the role of faith in our lives, we can unlock the potential to overcome anxiety, depression, self-sabotage, and overthinking.

The key lies in aligning ourselves with the infinite power that exists beyond our human understanding. As you progress, bear in mind the knowledge that your faith is a powerful force capable of transforming your life. By doing so, we can tap into the limitless energy that can solve our problems and bring us peace.

Thank you for embarking on this enlightening journey. May the wisdom shared in these pages lead you to live a life of purpose, serenity, and unshakeable faith.

AIC

Acknowledgement

I want to extend my heartfelt thanks to Furqan Qureshi. His unwavering dedication to researching the Quran and its deep connection to modern science, ancient history, and archaeology has greatly deepened the understanding of these fields and enriched faith in God. His unique perspective intricately connects faith and reason, the Quran and science. His work serves as a powerful reminder of how the Quran guides our understanding of the past, present, and future.

This book further extends his mission to help people understand the greatness and beauty of Allah and how much Allah loves us. I am deeply grateful to Furqan Qureshi for his generosity in sharing his research and insights with the world. It is an honor to base this book on his work.

Finally, I want to express my sincere gratitude to my family and parents. Their unwavering support and encouragement throughout the writing of this book have been invaluable. I am deeply thankful for their belief in the importance of this endeavor.

Made in the USA
Middletown, DE
25 June 2024